The G
according to John

AUTHORIZED VERSION

Arranged in paragraphs, with Old Testament references and index to the principal subjects

TRINITARIAN BIBLE SOCIETY
Tyndale House, Dorset Road,
London, SW19 3NN, England

10m/3/97

Printed in Great Britain at the University Press, Cambridge

The Gospel according to John

1 In the beginning was the Word, and the
Word was with God, and the Word was
God. 2The same was in the beginning with
God. 3All things were made by him; and
without him was not any thing made that was
made. 4In him was life; and the life was the
light of men. 5And the light shineth in dark-
ness; and the darkness comprehended it not.

6There was a man sent from God, whose
name *was* John. 7The same came for a witness,
to bear witness of the Light, that all *men*
through him might believe. 8He was not that
Light, but *was sent* to bear witness of that
Light.

9*That* was the true Light, which lighteth
every man that cometh into the world. 10He
was in the world, and the world was made by
him, and the world knew him not. 11He came
unto his own, and his own received him not.

12 But as many as received him, to them gave
he power to become the sons of God, *even* to
them that believe on his name: 13 Which were
born, not of blood, nor of the will of the flesh,
nor of the will of man, but of God.

14 And the Word was made flesh, and dwelt
among us, (and we beheld his glory, the glory
as of the only begotten of the Father,) full of
grace and truth.

15 John bare witness of him, and cried, say-
ing, This was he of whom I spake, He that
cometh after me is preferred before me: for
he was before me. 16 And of his fulness have all
we received, and grace for grace. 17 For the
law was given by Moses, *but* grace and truth
came by Jesus Christ. 18 No man hath seen
God at any time; the only begotten Son,
which is in the bosom of the Father, he hath
declared *him*.

The witness of John the Baptist

19 And this is the record of John, when the
Jews sent priests and Levites from Jerusalem

to ask him, Who art thou? [20]And he con-
fessed, and denied not; but confessed, I am
not the Christ. [21]And they asked him, What
then? Art thou Elias? And he saith, I am not.
Art thou that prophet? And he answered, No.
[22]Then said they unto him, Who art thou?
that we may give an answer to them that sent
us. What sayest thou of thyself?

[23]He said, I *am* the voice of one crying in
the wilderness, Make straight the way of
the Lord, as said the prophet Esaias. (*Isaiah
40.3*). [24]And they which were sent were of
the Pharisees. [25]And they asked him, and said
unto him, Why baptizest thou then, if thou
be not that Christ, nor Elias, neither that
prophet?

[26]John answered them, saying, I baptize
with water: but there standeth one among you,
whom ye know not; [27]He it is, who coming
after me is preferred before me, whose shoe's
latchet I am not worthy to unloose.

[28]These things were done in Bethabara be-
yond Jordan, where John was baptizing.

29 The next day John seeth Jesus coming
unto him, and saith, Behold the Lamb of God,
which taketh away the sin of the world. 30 This
is he of whom I said, After me cometh a man
which is preferred before me: for he was
before me. 31 And I knew him not: but that he
should be made manifest to Israel, therefore
am I come baptizing with water.

32 And John bare record, saying, I saw the
Spirit descending from heaven like a dove,
and it abode upon him. 33 And I knew him not:
but he that sent me to baptize with water, the
same said unto me, Upon whom thou shalt
see the Spirit descending, and remaining on
him, the same is he which baptizeth with the
Holy Ghost. 34 And I saw, and bare record
that this is the Son of God.

Disciples of Jesus

35 Again the next day after John stood, and two
of his disciples; 36 And looking upon Jesus as
he walked, he saith, Behold the Lamb of God!
37 And the two disciples heard him speak, and

they followed Jesus. 38 Then Jesus turned, and
saw them following, and saith unto them,
What seek ye? They said unto him, Rabbi,
(which is to say, being interpreted, Master,)
where dwellest thou? 39 He saith unto them,
Come and see. They came and saw where he
dwelt, and abode with him that day: for it was
about the tenth hour.

40 One of the two which heard John *speak*,
and followed him, was Andrew, Simon
Peter's brother. 41 He first findeth his own
brother Simon, and saith unto him, We have
found the Messias, which is, being inter-
preted, the Christ. 42 And he brought him to
Jesus. And when Jesus beheld him, he said,
Thou art Simon the son of Jona: thou shalt
be called Cephas, which is by interpretation,
A stone.

43 The day following Jesus would go forth
into Galilee, and findeth Philip, and saith un-
to him, Follow me. 44 Now Philip was of Beth-
saida, the city of Andrew and Peter.

45 Philip findeth Nathanael, and saith unto

him, We have found him, of whom Moses in
the law, and the prophets, did write, Jesus of
Nazareth, the son of Joseph. 46 And Nathanael
said unto him, Can there any good thing
come out of Nazareth? Philip saith unto him,
Come and see. 47 Jesus saw Nathanael coming
to him, and saith of him, Behold an Israelite
indeed, in whom is no guile! 48 Nathanael saith
unto him, Whence knowest thou me? Jesus
answered and said unto him, Before that
Philip called thee, when thou wast under the
fig tree, I saw thee.

49 Nathanael answered and saith unto him,
Rabbi, thou art the Son of God; thou art the
King of Israel. 50 Jesus answered and said un-
to him, Because I said unto thee, I saw thee
under the fig tree, believest thou? thou shalt see
greater things than these. 51 And he saith unto
him, Verily, verily, I say unto you, Hereafter
ye shall see heaven open, and the angels of
God ascending and descending upon the Son
of man.

JOHN 2

The miracle at Cana

2 And the third day there was a marriage
in Cana of Galilee; and the mother of
Jesus was there: 2And both Jesus was called,
and his disciples, to the marriage. 3And when
they wanted wine, the mother of Jesus saith
unto him, They have no wine. 4Jesus saith
unto her, Woman, what have I to do with
thee? mine hour is not yet come. 5His mother
saith unto the servants, Whatsoever he saith
unto you, do *it*.

6And there were set there six waterpots of
stone, after the manner of the purifying of the
Jews, containing two or three firkins apiece.
7Jesus saith unto them, Fill the waterpots with
water. And they filled them up to the brim.
8And he saith unto them, Draw out now, and
bear unto the governor of the feast. And they
bare *it*.

9When the ruler of the feast had tasted the
water that was made wine, and knew not
whence it was: (but the servants which drew
the water knew;) the governor of the feast

called the bridegroom, 10 And saith unto him,
Every man at the beginning doth set forth
good wine; and when men have well drunk,
then that which is worse: *but* thou hast kept
the good wine until now.
11 This beginning of miracles did Jesus in
Cana of Galilee, and manifested forth his
glory; and his disciples believed on him.
12 After this he went down to Capernaum, he,
and his mother, and his brethren, and his
disciples: and they continued there not many
days.

My Father's House

13 And the Jews' passover was at hand, and
Jesus went up to Jerusalem, 14 And found in
the temple those that sold oxen and sheep and
doves, and the changers of money sitting:
15 And when he had made a scourge of small
cords, he drove them all out of the temple,
and the sheep, and the oxen; and poured out
the changers' money, and overthrew the
tables; 16 And said unto them that sold doves,

Take these things hence; make not my
Father's house an house of merchandise.
17 And his disciples remembered that it was
written, The zeal of thine house hath eaten
me up. (*Psalm 69.9*).

18 Then answered the Jews and said unto
him, What sign shewest thou unto us, seeing
that thou doest these things? 19 Jesus an-
swered and said unto them, Destroy this tem-
ple, and in three days I will raise it up.
20 Then said the Jews, Forty and six years was
this temple in building, and wilt thou rear it
up in three days? 21 But he spake of the temple
of his body. 22 When therefore he was risen
from the dead, his disciples remembered that
he had said this unto them; and they be-
lieved the scripture, (*Psalm 16.10*) and the
word which Jesus had said.

23 Now when he was in Jerusalem at the
passover, in the feast *day*, many believed in
his name, when they saw the miracles which
he did. 24 But Jesus did not commit himself
unto them, because he knew all *men*, 25 And

needed not that any should testify of man: for
he knew what was in man.

Ye must be born again

3 There was a man of the Pharisees, named
Nicodemus, a ruler of the Jews: 2The
same came to Jesus by night, and said unto
him, Rabbi, we know that thou art a teacher
come from God: for no man can do these
miracles that thou doest, except God be with
him.
3Jesus answered and said unto him, Verily,
verily, I say unto thee, Except a man be born
again, he cannot see the kingdom of God.
4Nicodemus saith unto him, How can a man
be born when he is old? can he enter the
second time into his mother's womb, and be
born?
5Jesus answered, Verily, verily, I say unto
thee, Except a man be born of water and *of*
the Spirit, he cannot enter into the kingdom
of God. 6That which is born of the flesh is
flesh; and that which is born of the Spirit is

spirit. [7]Marvel not that I said unto thee, Ye
must be born again. [8]The wind bloweth where
it listeth, and thou hearest the sound thereof,
but canst not tell whence it cometh, and
whither it goeth: so is every one that is born
of the Spirit. [9]Nicodemus answered and said
unto him, How can these things be?

[10]Jesus answered and said unto him, Art
thou a master of Israel, and knowest not these
things? [11]Verily, verily, I say unto thee, We
speak that we do know, and testify that we
have seen; and ye receive not our witness.
[12]If I have told you earthly things, and ye
believe not, how shall ye believe, if I tell you
of heavenly things? [13]And no man hath as-
cended up to heaven, but he that came down
from heaven, *even* the Son of man which is in
heaven.

[14]And as Moses lifted up the serpent in the
wilderness, (*Numbers 21.9*) even so must
the Son of man be lifted up: [15]That whosoever
believeth in him should not perish, but have
eternal life. [16]For God so loved the world,

that he gave his only begotten Son, that who-
soever believeth in him should not perish,
but have everlasting life. 17For God sent not
his Son into the world to condemn the world;
but that the world through him might be
saved. 18He that believeth on him is not con-
demned: but he that believeth not is con-
demned already, because he hath not believed
in the name of the only begotten Son of God.
19And this is the condemnation, that light is
come into the world, and men loved darkness
rather than light, because their deeds were
evil. 20For every one that doeth evil hateth the
light, neither cometh to the light, lest his
deeds should be reproved. 21But he that doeth
truth cometh to the light, that his deeds may
be made manifest, that they are wrought in
God.

22After these things came Jesus and his
disciples into the land of Judæa; and there he
tarried with them, and baptized. 23And John
also was baptizing in Ænon near to Salim,

because there was much water there: and
they came, and were baptized. 24 For John was
not yet cast into prison. 25 Then there arose a
question between *some* of John's disciples and
the Jews about purifying. 26 And they came
unto John, and said unto him, Rabbi, he that
was with thee beyond Jordan, to whom thou
barest witness, behold, the same baptizeth,
and all *men* come to him. 27 John answered
and said, A man can receive nothing, except
it be given him from heaven. 28 Ye yourselves
bear me witness, that I said, I am not the
Christ, but that I am sent before him. 29 He
that hath the bride is the bridegroom: but the
friend of the bridegroom, which standeth and
heareth him, rejoiceth greatly because of the
bridegroom's voice: this my joy therefore is
fulfilled. 30 He must increase, but I *must* de-
crease. 31 He that cometh from above is above
all: he that is of the earth is earthly, and
speaketh of the earth: he that cometh from
heaven is above all. 32 And what he hath seen
and heard, that he testifieth; and no man re-

ceiveth his testimony. [33]He that hath received
his testimony hath set to his seal that God is
true. [34]For he whom God hath sent speaketh
the words of God: for God giveth not the
Spirit by measure *unto him*. (*Deuteronomy*
18.18). [35]The Father loveth the Son, and hath
given all things into his hand. [36]He that be-
lieveth on the Son hath everlasting life: and
he that believeth not the Son shall not see
life; but the wrath of God abideth on him.

Jesus in Samaria

4 When therefore the Lord knew how the
Pharisees had heard that Jesus made and
baptized more disciples than John, [2](Though
Jesus himself baptized not, but his disciples,)
[3]He left Judæa, and departed again into Gali-
lee.

[4]And he must needs go through Samaria.
[5]Then cometh he to a city of Samaria, which
is called Sychar, near to the parcel of ground
that Jacob gave to his son Joseph. [6]Now
Jacob's well was there. Jesus therefore, being

wearied with *his* journey, sat thus on the well:
and it was about the sixth hour.
7 There cometh a woman of Samaria to draw
water: Jesus saith unto her, Give me to drink.
8 (For his disciples were gone away unto the
city to buy meat.) 9 Then saith the woman of
Samaria unto him, How is it that thou, being
a Jew, askest drink of me, which am a woman
of Samaria? for the Jews have no dealings
with the Samaritans.
10 Jesus answered and said unto her, If thou
knewest the gift of God, and who it is that
saith to thee, Give me to drink; thou wouldest
have asked of him, and he would have given
thee living water. 11 The woman saith unto
him, Sir, thou hast nothing to draw with, and
the well is deep: from whence then hast thou
that living water? 12 Art thou greater than our
father Jacob, which gave us the well, and
drank thereof himself, and his children, and
his cattle?
13 Jesus answered and said unto her, Whoso-
ever drinketh of this water shall thirst again:

14 But whosoever drinketh of the water that I
shall give him shall never thirst; but the
water that I shall give him shall be in him a
well of water springing up into everlasting life.
15 The woman saith unto him, Sir, give me this
water, that I thirst not, neither come hither to
draw. 16 Jesus saith unto her, Go, call thy hus-
band, and come hither. 17 The woman an-
swered and said, I have no husband. Jesus
said unto her, Thou hast well said, I have no
husband: 18 For thou hast had five husbands;
and he whom thou now hast is not thy hus-
band: in that saidst thou truly. 19 The woman
saith unto him, Sir, I perceive that thou art a
prophet. 20 Our fathers worshipped in this
mountain; and ye say, that in Jerusalem is the
place where men ought to worship. 21 Jesus
saith unto her, Woman, believe me, the hour
cometh, when ye shall neither in this moun-
tain, nor yet at Jerusalem, worship the Father.
22 Ye worship ye know not what: we know
what we worship: for salvation is of the Jews.
23 But the hour cometh, and now is, when the

true worshippers shall worship the Father in
spirit and in truth: for the Father seeketh
such to worship him. 24God *is* a Spirit: and
they that worship him must worship *him* in
spirit and in truth. 25The woman saith unto
him, I know that Messias cometh, which is
called Christ: when he is come, he will tell us
all things. 26Jesus saith unto her, I that speak
unto thee am *he*.

27And upon this came his disciples, and
marvelled that he talked with the woman:
yet no man said, What seekest thou? or,
Why talkest thou with her? 28The woman
then left her waterpot, and went her way into
the city, and saith to the men, 29Come, see a
man, which told me all things that ever I did:
is not this the Christ? 30Then they went out of
the city, and came unto him.

31In the mean while his disciples prayed
him, saying, Master, eat. 32But he said unto
them, I have meat to eat that ye know not of.
33Therefore said the disciples one to another,
Hath any man brought him *ought* to eat?

34 Jesus saith unto them, My meat is to do the
will of him that sent me, and to finish his
work. 35 Say not ye, There are yet four months,
and *then* cometh harvest? behold, I say unto
you, Lift up your eyes, and look on the fields;
for they are white already to harvest. 36 And he
that reapeth receiveth wages, and gathereth
fruit unto life eternal: that both he that
soweth and he that reapeth may rejoice to-
gether. 37 And herein is that saying true, One
soweth, and another reapeth. 38 I sent you to
reap that whereon ye bestowed no labour:
other men laboured, and ye are entered into
their labours.

39 And many of the Samaritans of that city
believed on him for the saying of the woman,
which testified, He told me all that ever I did.
40 So when the Samaritans were come unto
him, they besought him that he would tarry
with them: and he abode there two days.
41 And many more believed because of his own
word; 42 And said unto the woman, Now we
believe, not because of thy saying: for we have

heard *him* ourselves, and know that this is in-
deed the Christ, the Saviour of the world.

A nobleman's son healed

[43]Now after two days he departed thence, and
went into Galilee. [44]For Jesus himself testified,
that a prophet hath no honour in his own
country. [45]Then when he was come into Gali-
lee, the Galilæans received him, having seen
all the things that he did at Jerusalem at the
feast: for they also went unto the feast.

[46]So Jesus came again into Cana of Galilee,
where he made the water wine. And there
was a certain nobleman, whose son was sick
at Capernaum. [47]When he heard that Jesus
was come out of Judæa into Galilee, he went
unto him, and besought him that he would
come down, and heal his son: for he was at the
point of death. [48]Then said Jesus unto him,
Except ye see signs and wonders, ye will not
believe. [49]The nobleman saith unto him, Sir,
come down ere my child die. [50]Jesus saith un-
to him, Go thy way; thy son liveth. And the

man believed the word that Jesus had spoken
unto him, and he went his way. 51 And as he
was now going down, his servants met him,
and told *him*, saying, Thy son liveth. 52 Then
enquired he of them the hour when he began
to amend. And they said unto him, Yesterday
at the seventh hour the fever left him. 53 So the
father knew that *it was* at the same hour, in
the which Jesus said unto him, Thy son
liveth: and himself believed, and his whole
house.

54 This *is* again the second miracle *that* Jesus
did, when he was come out of Judæa into
Galilee.

Jesus at the pool of Bethesda

5 After this there was a feast of the Jews;
and Jesus went up to Jerusalem.

2 Now there is at Jerusalem by the sheep
market a pool, which is called in the Hebrew
tongue Bethesda, having five porches. 3 In
these lay a great multitude of impotent folk, of
blind, halt, withered, waiting for the moving

of the water. [4]For an angel went down at a
certain season into the pool, and troubled the
water: whosoever then first after the troubling
of the water stepped in was made whole of
whatsoever disease he had.

[5]And a certain man was there, which had
an infirmity thirty and eight years. [6]When
Jesus saw him lie, and knew that he had been
now a long time *in that case*, he saith unto
him, Wilt thou be made whole? [7]The impo-
tent man answered him, Sir, I have no man,
when the water is troubled, to put me into the
pool: but while I am coming, another step-
peth down before me. [8]Jesus saith unto him,
Rise, take up thy bed, and walk. [9]And imme-
diately the man was made whole, and took up
his bed, and walked: and on the same day
was the sabbath.

[10]The Jews therefore said unto him that was
cured, It is the sabbath day: it is not lawful
for thee to carry *thy* bed. [11]He answered them,
He that made me whole, the same said unto
me, Take up thy bed, and walk. [12]Then asked

they him, What man is that which said unto
thee, Take up thy bed, and walk? 13 And he
that was healed wist not who it was: for Jesus
had conveyed himself away, a multitude being
in *that* place.

14 Afterward Jesus findeth him in the temple,
and said unto him, Behold, thou art made
whole: sin no more, lest a worse thing come
unto thee. 15 The man departed, and told the
Jews that it was Jesus, which had made him
whole. 16 And therefore did the Jews persecute
Jesus, and sought to slay him, because he had
done these things on the sabbath day.

17 But Jesus answered them, My Father
worketh hitherto, and I work. 18 Therefore
the Jews sought the more to kill him, because
he not only had broken the sabbath, but said
also that God was his Father, making himself
equal with God.

19 Then answered Jesus and said unto them,
Verily, verily, I say unto you, The Son can do
nothing of himself, but what he seeth the
Father do: for what things soever he doeth,

these also doeth the Son likewise. [20]For the
Father loveth the Son, and sheweth him all
things that himself doeth: and he will shew
him greater works than these, that ye may
marvel. [21]For as the Father raiseth up the
dead, and quickeneth *them;* even so the Son
quickeneth whom he will. [22]For the Father
judgeth no man, but hath committed all judg-
ment unto the Son: [23]That all *men* should
honour the Son, even as they honour the
Father. He that honoureth not the Son
honoureth not the Father which hath sent
him.

[24]Verily, verily, I say unto you, He that
heareth my word, and believeth on him that
sent me, hath everlasting life, and shall not
come into condemnation; but is passed from
death unto life. [25]Verily, verily, I say unto you,
The hour is coming, and now is, when the
dead shall hear the voice of the Son of God:
and they that hear shall live. [26]For as the
Father hath life in himself; so hath he given
to the Son to have life in himself; [27]And hath

given him authority to execute judgment also,
because he is the Son of man. [28]Marvel not at
this: for the hour is coming, in the which all
that are in the graves shall hear his voice,
[29]And shall come forth; they that have done
good, unto the resurrection of life; and they
that have done evil, unto the resurrection of
damnation. (*Daniel 12.2*). [30]I can of mine own
self do nothing: as I hear, I judge: and my
judgment is just; because I seek not mine own
will, but the will of the Father which hath
sent me.

[31]If I bear witness of myself, my witness is
not true. [32]There is another that beareth wit-
ness of me; and I know that the witness which
he witnesseth of me is true. [33]Ye sent unto
John, and he bare witness unto the truth.
[34]But I receive not testimony from man: but
these things I say, that ye might be saved.
[35]He was a burning and a shining light: and
ye were willing for a season to rejoice in his
light. [36]But I have greater witness than *that*
of John: for the works which the Father hath

given me to finish, the same works that I do,
bear witness of me, that the Father hath sent
me.
[37]And the Father himself, which hath sent
me, hath borne witness of me. Ye have neither
heard his voice at any time, nor seen his
shape. [38]And ye have not his word abiding in
you: for whom he hath sent, him ye believe
not. [39]Search the scriptures; for in them ye
think ye have eternal life: and they are they
which testify of me. [40]And ye will not come
to me, that ye might have life.
[41]I receive not honour from men. [42]But I
know you, that ye have not the love of God in
you. [43]I am come in my Father's name, and
ye receive me not: if another shall come in his
own name, him ye will receive. [44]How can ye
believe, which receive honour one of another,
and seek not the honour that *cometh* from
God only? [45]Do not think that I will accuse
you to the Father: there is *one* that accuseth
you, *even* Moses, in whom ye trust. [46]For had
ye believed Moses, ye would have believed

me: for he wrote of me. [47]But if ye believe not
his writings, how shall ye believe my words?

The miracle of the loaves and fishes

6 After these things Jesus went over the
sea of Galilee, which is *the sea* of Tibe-
rias. [2]And a great multitude followed him,
because they saw his miracles which he did
on them that were diseased. [3]And Jesus went
up into a mountain, and there he sat with his
disciples.

[4]And the passover, a feast of the Jews, was
nigh.

[5]When Jesus then lifted up *his* eyes, and
saw a great company come unto him, he
saith unto Philip, Whence shall we buy bread,
that these may eat? [6]And this he said to prove
him: for he himself knew what he would do.
[7]Philip answered him, Two hundred penny-
worth of bread is not sufficient for them, that
every one of them may take a little. [8]One of
his disciples, Andrew, Simon Peter's brother,
saith unto him, [9]There is a lad here, which

hath five barley loaves, and two small fishes:
but what are they among so many? 10And
Jesus said, Make the men sit down. Now
there was much grass in the place. So the men
sat down, in number about five thousand.

11And Jesus took the loaves; and when he
had given thanks, he distributed to the dis-
ciples, and the disciples to them that were set
down; and likewise of the fishes as much as
they would. 12When they were filled, he said
unto his disciples, Gather up the fragments
that remain, that nothing be lost. 13Therefore
they gathered *them* together, and filled twelve
baskets with the fragments of the five barley
loaves, which remained over and above unto
them that had eaten.

14Then those men, when they had seen the
miracle that Jesus did, said, This is of a truth
that prophet that should come into the world.
(*Deuteronomy 18.18*). 15When Jesus therefore
perceived that they would come and take him
by force, to make him a king, he departed
again into a mountain himself alone.

16 And when even was *now* come, his dis-
ciples went down unto the sea, 17 And entered
into a ship, and went over the sea toward
Capernaum. And it was now dark, and Jesus
was not come to them. 18 And the sea arose by
reason of a great wind that blew. 19 So when
they had rowed about five and twenty or
thirty furlongs, they see Jesus walking on the
sea, and drawing nigh unto the ship: and they
were afraid. 20 But he saith unto them, It is I;
be not afraid. 21 Then they willingly received
him into the ship: and immediately the ship
was at the land whither they went.

The Bread of Life

22 The day following, when the people which
stood on the other side of the sea saw that
there was none other boat there, save that one
whereinto his disciples were entered, and that
Jesus went not with his disciples into the boat,
but *that* his disciples were gone away alone;
23 (Howbeit there came other boats from Ti-
berias nigh unto the place where they did eat

bread, after that the Lord had given thanks:)
[24]When the people therefore saw that Jesus
was not there, neither his disciples, they also
took shipping, and came to Capernaum, seek-
ing for Jesus. [25]And when they had found him
on the other side of the sea, they said unto
him, Rabbi, when camest thou hither?
[26]Jesus answered them and said, Verily,
verily, I say unto you, Ye seek me, not be-
cause ye saw the miracles, but because ye did
eat of the loaves, and were filled. [27]Labour not
for the meat which perisheth, but for that meat
which endureth unto everlasting life, which
the Son of man shall give unto you: for him
hath God the Father sealed.
[28]Then said they unto him, What shall we
do, that we might work the works of God?
[29]Jesus answered and said unto them, This is
the work of God, that ye believe on him
whom he hath sent. [30]They said therefore un-
to him, What sign shewest thou then, that we
may see, and believe thee? what dost thou
work? [31]Our fathers did eat manna in the

desert; as it is written, He gave them bread
from heaven to eat. (*Psalm 78.24*).
32 Then Jesus said unto them, Verily, verily,
I say unto you, Moses gave you not that
bread from heaven; but my Father giveth you
the true bread from heaven. 33 For the bread
of God is he which cometh down from heaven,
and giveth life unto the world. 34 Then said they
unto him, Lord, evermore give us this bread.
35 And Jesus said unto them, I am the bread
of life: he that cometh to me shall never hun-
ger; and he that believeth on me shall never
thirst. 36 But I said unto you, That ye also have
seen me, and believe not. 37 All that the Father
giveth me shall come to me; and him that
cometh to me I will in no wise cast out. 38 For
I came down from heaven, not to do mine
own will, but the will of him that sent me.
39 And this is the Father's will which hath sent
me, that of all which he hath given me I
should lose nothing, but should raise it up
again at the last day. 40 And this is the will of
him that sent me, that every one which seeth

the Son, and believeth on him, may have ever-
lasting life: and I will raise him up at the last
day. 41The Jews then murmured at him, be-
cause he said, I am the bread which came
down from heaven. 42And they said, Is not
this Jesus, the son of Joseph, whose father and
mother we know? how is it then that he saith,
I came down from heaven?

43Jesus therefore answered and said unto
them, Murmur not among yourselves. 44No
man can come to me, except the Father which
hath sent me draw him: and I will raise him
up at the last day. 45It is written in the pro-
phets, And they shall be all taught of God.
(*Isaiah 54.13*). Every man therefore that
hath heard, and hath learned of the Father,
cometh unto me. 46Not that any man hath
seen the Father, save he which is of God, he
hath seen the Father. 47Verily, verily, I say
unto you, He that believeth on me hath ever-
lasting life. 48I am that bread of life. 49Your
fathers did eat manna in the wilderness, and
are dead. 50This is the bread which cometh

down from heaven, that a man may eat there-
of, and not die. 51 I am the living bread which
came down from heaven: if any man eat of
this bread, he shall live for ever: and the bread
that I will give is my flesh, which I will give
for the life of the world.

52 The Jews therefore strove among them-
selves, saying, How can this man give us *his*
flesh to eat? 53 Then Jesus said unto them,
Verily, verily, I say unto you, Except ye eat
the flesh of the Son of man, and drink his
blood, ye have no life in you. 54 Whoso eateth
my flesh, and drinketh my blood, hath eternal
life; and I will raise him up at the last day.
55 For my flesh is meat indeed, and my blood is
drink indeed. 56 He that eateth my flesh, and
drinketh my blood, dwelleth in me, and I in
him. 57 As the living Father hath sent me, and
I live by the Father: so he that eateth me, even
he shall live by me. 58 This is that bread which
came down from heaven: not as your fathers
did eat manna, and are dead: he that eateth
of this bread shall live for ever.

59 These things said he in the synagogue, as
he taught in Capernaum.

60 Many therefore of his disciples, when they
had heard *this*, said, This is an hard saying;
who can hear it? 61 When Jesus knew in him-
self that his disciples murmured at it, he said
unto them, Doth this offend you? 62 *What*
and if ye shall see the Son of man ascend up
where he was before? 63 It is the spirit that
quickeneth; the flesh profiteth nothing: the
words that I speak unto you, *they* are spirit,
and *they* are life. 64 But there are some of you
that believe not. For Jesus knew from the
beginning who they were that believed not,
and who should betray him. 65 And he said,
Therefore said I unto you, that no man can
come unto me, except it were given unto him
of my Father.

66 From that *time* many of his disciples went
back, and walked no more with him. 67 Then
said Jesus unto the twelve, Will ye also go
away? 68 Then Simon Peter answered him,
Lord, to whom shall we go? thou hast the

words of eternal life. 69 And we believe and are
sure that thou art that Christ, the Son of the
living God. 70 Jesus answered them, Have not
I chosen you twelve, and one of you is a devil?
71 He spake of Judas Iscariot *the son* of Simon:
for he it was that should betray him, being one
of the twelve.

Jesus opposed by the Jews

7 After these things Jesus walked in Gali-
lee: for he would not walk in Jewry,
because the Jews sought to kill him.

2 Now the Jews' feast of tabernacles was at
hand. 3 His brethren therefore said unto him,
Depart hence, and go into Judæa, that thy
disciples also may see the works that thou
doest. 4 For *there is* no man *that* doeth any
thing in secret, and he himself seeketh to be
known openly. If thou do these things, shew
thyself to the world. 5 For neither did his
brethren believe in him.

6 Then Jesus said unto them, My time is not
yet come: but your time is alway ready. 7 The

world cannot hate you; but me it hateth, be-
cause I testify of it, that the works thereof are
evil. [8]Go ye up unto this feast: I go not up yet
unto this feast; for my time is not yet full
come. [9]When he had said these words unto
them, he abode *still* in Galilee. [10]But when his
brethren were gone up, then went he also up
unto the feast, not openly, but as it were in
secret.

[11]Then the Jews sought him at the feast, and
said, Where is he? [12]And there was much
murmuring among the people concerning
him: for some said, He is a good man: others
said, Nay; but he deceiveth the people. [13]How-
beit no man spake openly of him for fear of
the Jews.

[14]Now about the midst of the feast Jesus
went up into the temple, and taught. [15]And
the Jews marvelled, saying, How knoweth
this man letters, having never learned? [16]Jesus
answered them, and said, My doctrine is not
mine, but his that sent me. [17]If any man will
do his will, he shall know of the doctrine,

whether it be of God, or *whether* I speak of
myself. [18]He that speaketh of himself seeketh
his own glory: but he that seeketh his glory
that sent him, the same is true, and no un-
righteousness is in him. [19]Did not Moses give
you the law, and *yet* none of you keepeth the
law? Why go ye about to kill me?
[20]The people answered and said, Thou hast
a devil: who goeth about to kill thee? [21]Jesus
answered and said unto them, I have done
one work, and ye all marvel. [22]Moses therefore
gave unto you circumcision; (not because it is
of Moses, but of the fathers;) and ye on the
sabbath day circumcise a man. [23]If a man on
the sabbath day receive circumcision, that the
law of Moses should not be broken; are ye
angry at me, because I have made a man every
whit whole on the sabbath day? [24]Judge not
according to the appearance, but judge right-
eous judgment.
[25]Then said some of them of Jerusalem, Is
not this he, whom they seek to kill? [26]But, lo,
he speaketh boldly, and they say nothing

unto him. Do the rulers know indeed that this
is the very Christ? 27 Howbeit we know this
man whence he is: but when Christ cometh,
no man knoweth whence he is.

28 Then cried Jesus in the temple as he
taught, saying, Ye both know me, and ye
know whence I am: and I am not come of
myself, but he that sent me is true, whom ye
know not. 29 But I know him: for I am from
him, and he hath sent me. 30 Then they sought
to take him: but no man laid hands on him,
because his hour was not yet come.

31 And many of the people believed on him,
and said, When Christ cometh, will he do
more miracles than these which this *man* hath
done? 32 The Pharisees heard that the people
murmured such things concerning him; and
the Pharisees and the chief priests sent offi-
cers to take him.

33 Then said Jesus unto them, Yet a little
while am I with you, and *then* I go unto him
that sent me. 34 Ye shall seek me, and shall not
find *me:* and where I am, *thither* ye cannot

come. 35Then said the Jews among them-
selves, Whither will he go, that we shall not
find him? will he go unto the dispersed
among the Gentiles, and teach the Gentiles?
36What *manner of* saying is this that he said,
Ye shall seek me, and shall not find *me:* and
where I am, *thither* ye cannot come?

A division among the people

37In the last day, that great *day* of the feast,
Jesus stood and cried, saying, If any man
thirst, let him come unto me, and drink. 38He
that believeth on me, as the scripture hath
said, out of his belly shall flow rivers of living
water. 39(But this spake he of the Spirit, which
they that believe on him should receive: for
the Holy Ghost was not yet *given;* because
that Jesus was not yet glorified.) 40Many of
the people therefore, when they heard this
saying, said, Of a truth this is the Prophet.
41Others said, This is the Christ. But some
said, Shall Christ come out of Galilee? 42Hath
not the scripture said, That Christ cometh of

the seed of David, and out of the town of
Bethlehem, where David was? (*Micah 5.1*).
43 So there was a division among the people
because of him. 44 And some of them would
have taken him; but no man laid hands on
him.

45 Then came the officers to the chief priests
and Pharisees; and they said unto them, Why
have ye not brought him? 46 The officers an-
swered, Never man spake like this man.
47 Then answered them the Pharisees, Are ye
also deceived? 48 Have any of the rulers or of
the Pharisees believed on him? 49 But this
people who knoweth not the law are cursed.
50 Nicodemus saith unto them, (he that came
to Jesus by night, being one of them,) 51 Doth
our law judge *any* man, before it hear him,
and know what he doeth? 52 They answered
and said unto him, Art thou also of Galilee?
Search, and look: for out of Galilee ariseth no
prophet.

53 And every man went unto his own house.

8 Jesus went unto the mount of Olives.
2And early in the morning he came again
into the temple, and all the people came unto
him; and he sat down, and taught them.
3And the scribes and Pharisees brought un-
to him a woman taken in adultery; and when
they had set her in the midst, 4They say unto
him, Master, this woman was taken in adul-
tery, in the very act. 5Now Moses in the law
commanded us, that such should be stoned:
but what sayest thou? 6This they said, tempt-
ing him, that they might have to accuse him.
But Jesus stooped down, and with *his* finger
wrote on the ground, *as though he heard them
not*. 7So when they continued asking him, he
lifted up himself, and said unto them, He that
is without sin among you, let him first cast a
stone at her. 8And again he stooped down, and
wrote on the ground. 9And they which heard
it, being convicted by *their own* conscience,
went out one by one, beginning at the eldest,
even unto the last: and Jesus was left alone,
and the woman standing in the midst. 10When

Jesus had lifted up himself, and saw none but
the woman, he said unto her, Woman, where
are those thine accusers? hath no man con-
demned thee? 11She said, No man, Lord.
And Jesus said unto her, Neither do I con-
demn thee: go, and sin no more.

The Light of the World

12Then spake Jesus again unto them, saying, I
am the light of the world: he that followeth me
shall not walk in darkness, but shall have the
light of life.

13The Pharisees therefore said unto him,
Thou bearest record of thyself; thy record is
not true. 14Jesus answered and said unto them,
Though I bear record of myself, *yet* my re-
cord is true: for I know whence I came, and
whither I go; but ye cannot tell whence I
come, and whither I go. 15Ye judge after the
flesh; I judge no man. 16And yet if I judge,
my judgment is true: for I am not alone, but I
and the Father that sent me. 17It is also written
in your law, that the testimony of two men is

true. (*Deuteronomy 19.15*). [18]I am one that
bear witness of myself, and the Father that
sent me beareth witness of me. [19]Then said
they unto him, Where is thy Father? Jesus
answered, Ye neither know me, nor my
Father: if ye had known me, ye should
have known my Father also.

[20]These words spake Jesus in the treasury,
as he taught in the temple: and no man laid
hands on him; for his hour was not yet come.

[21]Then said Jesus again unto them, I go my
way, and ye shall seek me, and shall die in
your sins: whither I go, ye cannot come.
[22]Then said the Jews, Will he kill himself?
because he saith, Whither I go, ye cannot
come.

[23]And he said unto them, Ye are from be-
neath; I am from above: ye are of this world;
I am not of this world. [24]I said therefore unto
you, that ye shall die in your sins: for if ye
believe not that I am *he*, ye shall die in your
sins.

[25]Then said they unto him, Who art thou?

And Jesus saith unto them, Even *the same*
that I said unto you from the beginning. 26I
have many things to say and to judge of you:
but he that sent me is true; and I speak to the
world those things which I have heard of him.
27They understood not that he spake to them
of the Father.

28Then said Jesus unto them, When ye have
lifted up the Son of man, then shall ye know
that I am *he*, and *that* I do nothing of myself;
but as my Father hath taught me, I speak
these things. 29And he that sent me is with me:
the Father hath not left me alone; for I do
always those things that please him.

Jesus is before Abraham

30As he spake these words, many believed on
him. 31Then said Jesus to those Jews which
believed on him, If ye continue in my word,
then are ye my disciples indeed; 32And ye shall
know the truth, and the truth shall make you
free. 33They answered him, We be Abraham's
seed, and were never in bondage to any man:

how sayest thou, Ye shall be made free?
34 Jesus answered them, Verily, verily, I say
unto you, Whosoever committeth sin is the
servant of sin. 35 And the servant abideth not
in the house for ever: *but* the Son abideth
ever. 36 If the Son therefore shall make you
free, ye shall be free indeed. 37 I know that ye
are Abraham's seed; but ye seek to kill me,
because my word hath no place in you. 38 I
speak that which I have seen with my Father:
and ye do that which ye have seen with your
father.

39 They answered and said unto him, Abra-
ham is our father. Jesus saith unto them, If ye
were Abraham's children, ye would do the
works of Abraham. 40 But now ye seek to kill
me, a man that hath told you the truth, which
I have heard of God: this did not Abraham.
41 Ye do the deeds of your father. Then said
they to him, We be not born of fornication;
we have one Father, *even* God. 42 Jesus said
unto them, If God were your Father, ye would
love me: for I proceeded forth and came from

God; neither came I of myself, but he sent me.
43Why do ye not understand my speech? *even*
because ye cannot hear my word. 44Ye are of
your father the devil, and the lusts of your
father ye will do. He was a murderer from the
beginning, and abode not in the truth, be-
cause there is no truth in him. When he
speaketh a lie, he speaketh of his own: for he
is a liar, and the father of it. 45And because I
tell *you* the truth, ye believe me not. 46Which
of you convinceth me of sin? And if I say the
truth, why do ye not believe me? 47He that is
of God heareth God's words: ye therefore
hear *them* not, because ye are not of God.

48Then answered the Jews, and said unto
him, Say we not well that thou art a Samaritan,
and hast a devil? 49Jesus answered, I have not
a devil; but I honour my Father, and ye do
dishonour me. 50And I seek not mine own
glory: there is one that seeketh and judgeth.
51Verily, verily, I say unto you, If a man keep
my saying, he shall never see death. 52Then
said the Jews unto him, Now we know that

thou hast a devil. Abraham is dead, and the
prophets; and thou sayest, If a man keep my
saying, he shall never taste of death. 53Art thou
greater than our father Abraham, which is
dead? and the prophets are dead: whom
makest thou thyself?

54Jesus answered, If I honour myself, my
honour is nothing: it is my Father that
honoureth me; of whom ye say, that he is
your God: 55Yet ye have not known him; but
I know him: and if I should say, I know him
not, I shall be a liar like unto you: but I know
him, and keep his saying. 56Your father Abra-
ham rejoiced to see my day: and he saw *it*,
and was glad. 57Then said the Jews unto him,
Thou art not yet fifty years old, and hast thou
seen Abraham? 58Jesus said unto them, Verily,
verily, I say unto you, Before Abraham was,
I am.

59Then took they up stones to cast at him:
but Jesus hid himself, and went out of the
temple, going through the midst of them, and
so passed by.

Jesus heals a man born blind

9 And as *Jesus* passed by, he saw a man
which was blind from *his* birth. [2]And
his disciples asked him, saying, Master, who
did sin, this man, or his parents, that he was
born blind? [3]Jesus answered, Neither hath
this man sinned, nor his parents: but that the
works of God should be made manifest in
him. [4]I must work the works of him that sent
me, while it is day: the night cometh, when no
man can work. [5]As long as I am in the world,
I am the light of the world.

[6]When he had thus spoken, he spat on the
ground, and made clay of the spittle, and he
anointed the eyes of the blind man with the
clay, [7]And said unto him, Go, wash in the
pool of Siloam, (which is by interpretation,
Sent.) He went his way therefore, and washed,
and came seeing. [8]The neighbours therefore,
and they which before had seen him that he
was blind, said, Is not this he that sat and
begged? [9]Some said, This is he: others *said*,
He is like him: *but* he said, I am *he*. [10]There-

fore said they unto him, How were thine eyes
opened? [11]He answered and said, A man that
is called Jesus made clay, and anointed mine
eyes, and said unto me, Go to the pool of
Siloam, and wash: and I went and washed,
and I received sight. [12]Then said they unto
him, Where is he? He said, I know not.

[13]They brought to the Pharisees him that
aforetime was blind. [14]And it was the sabbath
day when Jesus made the clay, and opened
his eyes. [15]Then again the Pharisees also asked
him how he had received his sight. He said
unto them, He put clay upon mine eyes, and I
washed, and do see. [16]Therefore said some of
the Pharisees, This man is not of God, be-
cause he keepeth not the sabbath day. Others
said, How can a man that is a sinner do such
miracles? And there was a division among
them. [17]They say unto the blind man again,
What sayest thou of him, that he hath opened
thine eyes? He said, He is a prophet.

[18]But the Jews did not believe concerning
him, that he had been blind, and received his

sight, until they called the parents of him that
had received his sight. [19]And they asked them,
saying, Is this your son, who ye say was born
blind? how then doth he now see? [20]His
parents answered them and said, We know
that this is our son, and that he was born
blind: [21]But by what means he now seeth, we
know not; or who hath opened his eyes, we
know not: he is of age; ask him: he shall
speak for himself. [22]These *words* spake his
parents, because they feared the Jews: for the
Jews had agreed already, that if any man did
confess that he was Christ, he should be put
out of the synagogue. [23]Therefore said his
parents, He is of age; ask him.

[24]Then again called they the man that was
blind, and said unto him, Give God the praise:
we know that this man is a sinner. [25]He an-
swered and said, Whether he be a sinner *or
no*, I know not: one thing I know, that,
whereas I was blind, now I see. [26]Then said
they to him again, What did he to thee? how
opened he thine eyes? [27]He answered them, I

have told you already, and ye did not hear:
wherefore would ye hear *it* again? will ye also
be his disciples? 28Then they reviled him, and
said, Thou art his disciple; but we are Moses'
disciples. 29We know that God spake unto
Moses: *as for* this *fellow*, we know not from
whence he is.
30The man answered and said unto them,
Why herein is a marvellous thing, that ye
know not from whence he is, and *yet* he hath
opened mine eyes. 31Now we know that God
heareth not sinners: but if any man be a wor-
shipper of God, and doeth his will, him he
heareth. 32Since the world began was it not
heard that any man opened the eyes of one
that was born blind. 33If this man were not of
God, he could do nothing. 34They answered
and said unto him, Thou wast altogether born
in sins, and dost thou teach us? And they cast
him out.
35Jesus heard that they had cast him out;
and when he had found him, he said unto
him, Dost thou believe on the Son of God?

[36]He answered and said, Who is he, Lord,
that I might believe on him? [37]And Jesus said
unto him, Thou hast both seen him, and it is
he that talketh with thee. [38]And he said, Lord,
I believe. And he worshipped him.

[39]And Jesus said, For judgment I am come
into this world, that they which see not might
see; and that they which see might be made
blind. [40]And *some* of the Pharisees which were
with him heard these words, and said unto
him, Are we blind also? [41]Jesus said unto
them, If ye were blind, ye should have no sin:
but now ye say, We see; therefore your sin
remaineth.

The Good Shepherd

10 Verily, verily, I say unto you, He
that entereth not by the door into the
sheepfold, but climbeth up some other way,
the same is a thief and a robber. [2]But he that
entereth in by the door is the shepherd of the
sheep. [3]To him the porter openeth; and the
sheep hear his voice: and he calleth his own

sheep by name, and leadeth them out. 4And
when he putteth forth his own sheep, he goeth
before them, and the sheep follow him: for
they know his voice. 5And a stranger will they
not follow, but will flee from him: for they
know not the voice of strangers.

6This parable spake Jesus unto them: but
they understood not what things they were
which he spake unto them. 7Then said Jesus
unto them again, Verily, verily, I say unto
you, I am the door of the sheep. 8All that ever
came before me are thieves and robbers: but
the sheep did not hear them. 9I am the door:
by me if any man enter in, he shall be saved,
and shall go in and out, and find pasture.
10The thief cometh not, but for to steal, and to
kill, and to destroy: I am come that they
might have life, and that they might have *it*
more abundantly.

11I am the good shepherd: the good shep-
herd giveth his life for the sheep. 12But he that
is an hireling, and not the shepherd, whose
own the sheep are not, seeth the wolf coming,

and leaveth the sheep, and fleeth: and the
wolf catcheth them, and scattereth the sheep.
[13]The hireling fleeth, because he is an hireling,
and careth not for the sheep. [14]I am the good
shepherd, and know my *sheep*, and am known
of mine. [15]As the Father knoweth me, even so
know I the Father: and I lay down my life for
the sheep. [16]And other sheep I have, which
are not of this fold: them also I must bring,
and they shall hear my voice; and there shall
be one fold, *and* one shepherd. (*Ezekiel
34.23*). [17]Therefore doth my Father love me,
because I lay down my life, that I might take
it again. [18]No man taketh it from me, but I lay
it down of myself. I have power to lay it down,
and I have power to take it again. This commandment have I received of my Father.

Jesus the Son of God

[19]There was a division therefore again among
the Jews for these sayings. [20]And many of
them said, He hath a devil, and is mad; why
hear ye him? [21]Others said, These are not the

words of him that hath a devil. Can a devil
open the eyes of the blind?
22 And it was at Jerusalem the feast of the
dedication, and it was winter. 23 And Jesus
walked in the temple in Solomon's porch.
24 Then came the Jews round about him, and
said unto him, How long dost thou make us
to doubt? If thou be the Christ, tell us plainly.
25 Jesus answered them, I told you, and ye
believed not: the works that I do in my
Father's name, they bear witness of me. 26 But
ye believe not, because ye are not of my
sheep, as I said unto you. 27 My sheep hear my
voice, and I know them, and they follow me:
28 And I give unto them eternal life; and they
shall never perish, neither shall any *man* pluck
them out of my hand. 29 My Father, which
gave *them* me, is greater than all; and no
man is able to pluck *them* out of my Father's
hand. 30 I and *my* Father are one.
31 Then the Jews took up stones again to
stone him. 32 Jesus answered them, Many good
works have I shewed you from my Father;

for which of those works do ye stone me?
33 The Jews answered him, saying, For a good
work we stone thee not; but for blasphemy;
and because that thou, being a man, makest
thyself God.

34 Jesus answered them, Is it not written in
your law, I said, Ye are gods? (*Psalm 82.6*).
35 If he called them gods, unto whom the word
of God came, and the scripture cannot be
broken; 36 Say ye of him, whom the Father
hath sanctified, and sent into the world, Thou
blasphemest; because I said, I am the Son of
God? 37 If I do not the works of my Father,
believe me not. 38 But if I do, though ye be-
lieve not me, believe the works: that ye may
know, and believe, that the Father *is* in me,
and I in him.

39 Therefore they sought again to take him:
but he escaped out of their hand,

40 And went away again beyond Jordan into
the place where John at first baptized; and
there he abode. 41 And many resorted unto
him, and said, John did no miracle: but all

things that John spake of this man were true.
42And many believed on him there.

Jesus the Resurrection and the Life

11 Now a certain *man* was sick, *named*
Lazarus, of Bethany, the town of Mary
and her sister Martha. 2(It was *that* Mary
which anointed the Lord with ointment, and
wiped his feet with her hair, whose brother
Lazarus was sick.) 3Therefore his sisters sent
unto him, saying, Lord, behold, he whom
thou lovest is sick. 4When Jesus heard *that*,
he said, This sickness is not unto death, but
for the glory of God, that the Son of God
might be glorified thereby.
5Now Jesus loved Martha, and her sister,
and Lazarus. 6When he had heard therefore
that he was sick, he abode two days still in the
same place where he was. 7Then after that
saith he to *his* disciples, Let us go into Judæa
again. 8*His* disciples say unto him, Master,
the Jews of late sought to stone thee; and
goest thou thither again?

9Jesus answered, Are there not twelve hours
in the day? If any man walk in the day, he
stumbleth not, because he seeth the light of
this world. 10But if a man walk in the night, he
stumbleth, because there is no light in him.
11These things said he: and after that he saith
unto them, Our friend Lazarus sleepeth; but
I go, that I may awake him out of sleep.

12Then said his disciples, Lord, if he sleep,
he shall do well. 13Howbeit Jesus spake of his
death: but they thought that he had spoken of
taking of rest in sleep. 14Then said Jesus unto
them plainly, Lazarus is dead. 15And I am
glad for your sakes that I was not there, to the
intent ye may believe; nevertheless let us go
unto him. 16Then said Thomas, which is called
Didymus, unto his fellow disciples, Let us
also go, that we may die with him.

17Then when Jesus came, he found that he
had *lain* in the grave four days already. 18Now
Bethany was nigh unto Jerusalem, about fif-
teen furlongs off: 19And many of the Jews
came to Martha and Mary, to comfort them

concerning their brother. [20]Then Martha, as
soon as she heard that Jesus was coming, went
and met him: but Mary sat *still* in the house.

[21]Then said Martha unto Jesus, Lord, if thou
hadst been here, my brother had not died.
[22]But I know, that even now, whatsoever thou
wilt ask of God, God will give *it* thee. [23]Jesus
saith unto her, Thy brother shall rise again.
[24]Martha saith unto him, I know that he shall
rise again in the resurrection at the last day.
[25]Jesus said unto her, I am the resurrection,
and the life: he that believeth in me, though
he were dead, yet shall he live: [26]And who-
soever liveth and believeth in me shall never
die. Believest thou this? [27]She saith unto him,
Yea, Lord: I believe that thou art the Christ,
the Son of God, which should come into the
world.

[28]And when she had so said, she went her
way, and called Mary her sister secretly, say-
ing, The Master is come, and calleth for thee.
[29]As soon as she heard *that*, she arose quickly,
and came unto him. [30]Now Jesus was not yet

come into the town, but was in that place
where Martha met him. 31 The Jews then which
were with her in the house, and comforted
her, when they saw Mary, that she rose up
hastily and went out, followed her, saying,
She goeth unto the grave to weep there.
32 Then when Mary was come where Jesus
was, and saw him, she fell down at his feet,
saying unto him, Lord, if thou hadst been
here, my brother had not died. 33 When Jesus
therefore saw her weeping, and the Jews also
weeping which came with her, he groaned
in the spirit, and was troubled, 34 And said,
Where have ye laid him? They said unto
him, Lord, come and see.
35 Jesus wept.
36 Then said the Jews, Behold how he loved
him! 37 And some of them said, Could not this
man, which opened the eyes of the blind, have
caused that even this man should not have died?
38 Jesus therefore again groaning in himself
cometh to the grave. It was a cave, and a
stone lay upon it. 39 Jesus said, Take ye away

the stone. Martha, the sister of him that was
dead, saith unto him, Lord, by this time he
stinketh: for he hath been *dead* four days.
40 Jesus saith unto her, Said I not unto thee,
that, if thou wouldest believe, thou shouldest
see the glory of God? 41 Then they took away
the stone *from the place* where the dead was
laid. And Jesus lifted up *his* eyes, and said,
Father, I thank thee that thou hast heard me.
42 And I knew that thou hearest me always:
but because of the people which stand by I
said *it*, that they may believe that thou hast
sent me. 43 And when he thus had spoken, he
cried with a loud voice, Lazarus, come forth.
44 And he that was dead came forth, bound
hand and foot with graveclothes: and his face
was bound about with a napkin. Jesus saith
unto them, Loose him, and let him go.

45 Then many of the Jews which came to
Mary, and had seen the things which Jesus
did, believed on him. 46 But some of them went
their ways to the Pharisees, and told them
what things Jesus had done.

The Chief Priests and Pharisees take counsel to put Jesus to death

47Then gathered the chief priests and the Pha-
risees a council, and said, What do we? for
this man doeth many miracles. 48If we let him
thus alone, all *men* will believe on him: and
the Romans shall come and take away both
our place and nation. 49And one of them,
named Caiaphas, being the high priest that
same year, said unto them, Ye know nothing
at all, 50Nor consider that it is expedient for
us, that one man should die for the people,
and that the whole nation perish not. 51And
this spake he not of himself: but being high
priest that year, he prophesied that Jesus
should die for that nation; 52And not for that
nation only, but that also he should gather to-
gether in one the children of God that were
scattered abroad. (*Isaiah 53.8; 49.6*).

53Then from that day forth they took coun-
sel together for to put him to death. 54Jesus
therefore walked no more openly among the
Jews; but went thence unto a country near to

the wilderness, into a city called Ephraim, and
there continued with his disciples.
55 And the Jews' passover was nigh at hand:
and many went out of the country up to Jeru-
salem before the passover, to purify them-
selves. 56 Then sought they for Jesus, and spake
among themselves, as they stood in the
temple, What think ye, that he will not come
to the feast? 57 Now both the chief priests and
the Pharisees had given a commandment,
that, if any man knew where he were, he
should shew *it*, that they might take him.

The Anointing

12 Then Jesus six days before the pass-
over came to Bethany, where Lazarus
was which had been dead, whom he raised
from the dead. 2 There they made him a sup-
per; and Martha served: but Lazarus was one
of them that sat at the table with him. 3 Then
took Mary a pound of ointment of spikenard,
very costly, and anointed the feet of Jesus,
and wiped his feet with her hair: and the house

was filled with the odour of the ointment.
4 Then saith one of his disciples, Judas Is-
cariot, Simon's *son*, which should betray him,
5 Why was not this ointment sold for three
hundred pence, and given to the poor? 6 This
he said, not that he cared for the poor; but
because he was a thief, and had the bag, and
bare what was put therein.

7 Then said Jesus, Let her alone: against the
day of my burying hath she kept this. 8 For
the poor always ye have with you; but me ye
have not always. 9 Much people of the Jews
therefore knew that he was there: and they
came not for Jesus' sake only, but that they
might see Lazarus also, whom he had raised
from the dead. 10 But the chief priests con-
sulted that they might put Lazarus also to
death; 11 Because that by reason of him many
of the Jews went away, and believed on Jesus.

12 On the next day much people that were
come to the feast, when they heard that Jesus
was coming to Jerusalem, 13 Took branches of
palm trees, and went forth to meet him, and

cried, Hosanna: Blessed *is* the King of Israel
that cometh in the name of the Lord. (*Psalm*
118.25, *26*).

[14]And Jesus, when he had found a young
ass, sat thereon; as it is written, [15]Fear not,
daughter of Sion: behold, thy King cometh,
sitting on an ass's colt. (*Zechariah 9.9*).
[16]These things understood not his disciples
at the first: but when Jesus was glorified, then
remembered they that these things were writ-
ten of him, and *that* they had done these
things unto him.

[17]The people therefore that was with him
when he called Lazarus out of his grave, and
raised him from the dead, bare record. [18]For
this cause the people also met him, for that
they heard that he had done this miracle.
[19]The Pharisees therefore said among them-
selves, Perceive ye how ye prevail nothing?
behold the world is gone after him.

[20]And there were certain Greeks among
them that came up to worship at the feast:
[21]The same came therefore to Philip, which

was of Bethsaida of Galilee, and desired him,
saying, Sir, we would see Jesus. 22Philip
cometh and telleth Andrew: and again Andrew and Philip tell Jesus.

23And Jesus answered them, saying, The
hour is come, that the Son of man should be
glorified. 24Verily, verily, I say unto you, Except a corn of wheat fall into the ground and
die, it abideth alone: but if it die, it bringeth
forth much fruit. 25He that loveth his life shall
lose it; and he that hateth his life in this world
shall keep it unto life eternal. 26If any man
serve me, let him follow me; and where I am,
there shall also my servant be: if any man serve
me, him will *my* Father honour. 27Now is my
soul troubled; and what shall I say? Father,
save me from this hour: but for this cause came
I unto this hour. 28Father, glorify thy name.

Then came there a voice from heaven, *saying*, I have both glorified *it*, and will glorify *it*
again.

29The people therefore, that stood by, and
heard *it*, said that it thundered: others said,

An angel spake to him. [30]Jesus answered and
said, This voice came not because of me, but
for your sakes. [31]Now is the judgment of this
world: now shall the prince of this world be
cast out. [32]And I, if I be lifted up from the
earth, will draw all *men* unto me. [33]This he
said, signifying what death he should die.

[34]The people answered him, We have heard
out of the law that Christ abideth for ever:
and how sayest thou, The Son of man must be
lifted up? who is this Son of man? [35]Then
Jesus said unto them, Yet a little while is the
light with you. Walk while ye have the light,
lest darkness come upon you: for he that
walketh in darkness knoweth not whither he
goeth. [36]While ye have light, believe in the
light, that ye may be the children of light.
These things spake Jesus, and departed, and
did hide himself from them.

A prophecy of Isaiah fulfilled

[37]But though he had done so many miracles
before them, yet they believed not on him:

38That the saying of Esaias the prophet might
be fulfilled, which he spake, Lord, who
hath believed our report? and to whom hath
the arm of the Lord been revealed? (*Isaiah
53.1*). 39Therefore they could not believe,
because that Esaias said again, 40He hath
blinded their eyes, and hardened their heart;
that they should not see with *their* eyes, nor
understand with *their* heart, and be convert-
ed, and I should heal them. 41These things
said Esaias, when he saw his glory, and spake
of him. (*Isaiah 6.1-10*).

42Nevertheless among the chief rulers also
many believed on him; but because of the
Pharisees they did not confess *him*, lest they
should be put out of the synagogue: 43For
they loved the praise of men more than the
praise of God.

44Jesus cried and said, He that believeth on
me, believeth not on me, but on him that sent
me. 45And he that seeth me seeth him that
sent me. 46I am come a light into the world,
that whosoever believeth on me should not

abide in darkness. [47]And if any man hear my
words, and believe not, I judge him not: for I
came not to judge the world, but to save the
world. [48]He that rejecteth me, and receiveth
not my words, hath one that judgeth him: the
word that I have spoken, the same shall judge
him in the last day. [49]For I have not spoken of
myself; but the Father which sent me, he gave
me a commandment, what I should say, and
what I should speak. (*Deuteronomy 18.18, 19*).
[50]And I know that his commandment is life
everlasting: whatsoever I speak therefore, even
as the Father said unto me, so I speak.

Jesus washes His disciples' feet

13 Now before the feast of the passover,
when Jesus knew that his hour was
come that he should depart out of this world
unto the Father, having loved his own which
were in the world, he loved them unto the end.
[2]And supper being ended, the devil having
now put into the heart of Judas Iscariot,
Simon's *son*, to betray him; [3]Jesus knowing

that the Father had given all things into his
hands, and that he was come from God, and
went to God; 4He riseth from supper, and laid
aside his garments; and took a towel, and
girded himself. 5After that he poureth water
into a bason, and began to wash the disciples'
feet, and to wipe *them* with the towel where-
with he was girded.
6Then cometh he to Simon Peter: and Peter
saith unto him, Lord, dost thou wash my
feet? 7Jesus answered and said unto him,
What I do thou knowest not now; but thou
shalt know hereafter. 8Peter saith unto him,
Thou shalt never wash my feet. Jesus an-
swered him, If I wash thee not, thou hast no
part with me. 9Simon Peter saith unto him,
Lord, not my feet only, but also *my* hands and
my head. 10Jesus saith to him, He that is
washed needeth not save to wash *his* feet, but
is clean every whit: and ye are clean, but not
all. 11For he knew who should betray him;
therefore said he, Ye are not all clean.
12So after he had washed their feet, and had

taken his garments, and was set down again,
he said unto them, Know ye what I have done
to you? 13 Ye call me Master and Lord: and ye
say well; for *so* I am. 14 If I then, *your* Lord
and Master, have washed your feet; ye also
ought to wash one another's feet. 15 For I have
given you an example, that ye should do as I
have done to you. 16 Verily, verily, I say unto
you, The servant is not greater than his lord;
neither he that is sent greater than he that sent
him. 17 If ye know these things, happy are ye
if ye do them.

18 I speak not of you all: I know whom I
have chosen: but that the scripture may be
fulfilled, He that eateth bread with me hath
lifted up his heel against me. (*Psalm 41.9*).
19 Now I tell you before it come, that, when it
is come to pass, ye may believe that I am *he*.
20 Verily, verily, I say unto you, He that re-
ceiveth whomsoever I send receiveth me; and
he that receiveth me receiveth him that sent
me.

Jesus foretells His betrayal

21When Jesus had thus said, he was troubled in
spirit, and testified, and said, Verily, verily, I
say unto you, that one of you shall betray me.
22Then the disciples looked one on another,
doubting of whom he spake. 23Now there was
leaning on Jesus' bosom one of his disciples,
whom Jesus loved. 24Simon Peter therefore
beckoned to him, that he should ask who it
should be of whom he spake. 25He then lying
on Jesus' breast saith unto him, Lord, who is
it? 26Jesus answered, He it is, to whom I shall
give a sop, when I have dipped *it*. And when
he had dipped the sop, he gave *it* to Judas
Iscariot, *the son* of Simon. 27And after the sop
Satan entered into him. Then said Jesus unto
him, That thou doest, do quickly. 28Now no
man at the table knew for what intent he
spake this unto him. 29For some *of them*
thought, because Judas had the bag, that Jesus
had said unto him, Buy *those things* that we
have need of against the feast; or, that he
should give something to the poor. 30He then

having received the sop went immediately
out: and it was night.
[31]Therefore, when he was gone out, Jesus
said, Now is the Son of man glorified, and
God is glorified in him. [32]If God be glorified
in him, God shall also glorify him in himself,
and shall straightway glorify him.
[33]Little children, yet a little while I am with
you. Ye shall seek me: and as I said unto the
Jews, Whither I go, ye cannot come; so now
I say to you. [34]A new commandment I give
unto you, That ye love one another; as I have
loved you, that ye also love one another.
[35]By this shall all *men* know that ye are my
disciples, if ye have love one to another.
[36]Simon Peter said unto him, Lord, whither
goest thou? Jesus answered him, Whither I
go, thou canst not follow me now; but thou
shalt follow me afterwards. [37]Peter said unto
him, Lord, why cannot I follow thee now?
I will lay down my life for thy sake. [38]Jesus
answered him, Wilt thou lay down thy life for
my sake? Verily, verily, I say unto thee, The

cock shall not crow, till thou hast denied me
thrice.

The Way, the Truth, and the Life

14 Let not your heart be troubled: ye
believe in God, believe also in me.
2 In my Father's house are many mansions:
if *it were* not *so*, I would have told you. I go
to prepare a place for you. 3 And if I go and
prepare a place for you, I will come again,
and receive you unto myself; that where I am,
there ye may be also. 4 And whither I go ye
know, and the way ye know.

5 Thomas saith unto him, Lord, we know
not whither thou goest; and how can we
know the way? 6 Jesus saith unto him, I am
the way, the truth, and the life: no man
cometh unto the Father, but by me. 7 If ye
had known me, ye should have known my
Father also: and from henceforth ye know
him, and have seen him.

8 Philip saith unto him, Lord, shew us the
Father, and it sufficeth us. 9 Jesus saith unto

him, Have I been so long time with you, and
yet hast thou not known me, Philip? he that
hath seen me hath seen the Father; and how
sayest thou *then*, Shew us the Father? 10 Be-
lievest thou not that I am in the Father, and
the Father in me? the words that I speak un-
to you I speak not of myself: but the Father
that dwelleth in me, he doeth the works.
11 Believe me that I *am* in the Father, and the
Father in me: or else believe me for the very
works' sake.

12 Verily, verily, I say unto you, He that
believeth on me, the works that I do shall he
do also; and greater *works* than these shall he
do; because I go unto my Father. 13 And
whatsoever ye shall ask in my name, that will
I do, that the Father may be glorified in the
Son. 14 If ye shall ask any thing in my name,
I will do *it*.

15 If ye love me, keep my commandments.
16 And I will pray the Father, and he shall give
you another Comforter, that he may abide
with you for ever; 17 *Even* the Spirit of truth;

whom the world cannot receive, because it
seeth him not, neither knoweth him: but ye
know him; for he dwelleth with you, and
shall be in you. [18]I will not leave you com-
fortless: I will come to you. [19]Yet a little while,
and the world seeth me no more; but ye see
me: because I live, ye shall live also. [20]At that
day ye shall know that I *am* in my Father, and
ye in me, and I in you. [21]He that hath my
commandments, and keepeth them, he it is
that loveth me: and he that loveth me shall be
loved of my Father, and I will love him, and
will manifest myself to him.

[22]Judas saith unto him, not Iscariot, Lord,
how is it that thou wilt manifest thyself unto
us, and not unto the world? [23]Jesus answered
and said unto him, If a man love me, he will
keep my words: and my Father will love him,
and we will come unto him, and make our
abode with him. [24]He that loveth me not
keepeth not my sayings: and the word which
ye hear is not mine, but the Father's which
sent me.

25 These things have I spoken unto you,
being *yet* present with you. 26 But the Com-
forter, *which is* the Holy Ghost, whom the
Father will send in my name, he shall teach
you all things, and bring all things to your re-
membrance, whatsoever I have said unto you.

27 Peace I leave with you, my peace I give
unto you: not as the world giveth, give I unto
you. Let not your heart be troubled, neither
let it be afraid.

28 Ye have heard how I said unto you, I go
away, and come *again* unto you. If ye loved
me, ye would rejoice, because I said, I go
unto the Father: for my Father is greater than
I. 29 And now I have told you before it come
to pass, that, when it is come to pass, ye
might believe.

30 Hereafter I will not talk much with you:
for the prince of this world cometh, and hath
nothing in me. 31 But that the world may know
that I love the Father; and as the Father gave
me commandment, even so I do. Arise, let us
go hence.

JOHN 15

The True Vine

15 I am the true vine, and my Father is
the husbandman. [2]Every branch in
me that beareth not fruit he taketh away: and
every *branch* that beareth fruit, he purgeth it,
that it may bring forth more fruit. [3]Now ye are
clean through the word which I have spoken
unto you. [4]Abide in me, and I in you. As the
branch cannot bear fruit of itself, except it
abide in the vine; no more can ye, except
ye abide in me. [5]I am the vine, ye *are* the
branches: He that abideth in me, and I in him,
the same bringeth forth much fruit: for with-
out me ye can do nothing. [6]If a man abide not
in me, he is cast forth as a branch, and is
withered; and men gather them, and cast
them into the fire, and they are burned. [7]If ye
abide in me, and my words abide in you, ye
shall ask what ye will, and it shall be done
unto you. [8]Herein is my Father glorified, that
ye bear much fruit; so shall ye be my dis-
ciples.

[9]As the Father hath loved me, so have I

loved you: continue ye in my love. 10If ye
keep my commandments, ye shall abide in
my love; even as I have kept my Father's
commandments, and abide in his love. 11These
things have I spoken unto you, that my joy
might remain in you, and *that* your joy might
be full.

12This is my commandment, That ye love
one another, as I have loved you. 13Greater
love hath no man than this, that a man lay
down his life for his friends. 14Ye are my
friends, if ye do whatsoever I command you.
15Henceforth I call you not servants; for the
servant knoweth not what his lord doeth: but
I have called you friends; for all things that I
have heard of my Father I have made known
unto you. 16Ye have not chosen me, but I have
chosen you, and ordained you, that ye should
go and bring forth fruit, and *that* your fruit
should remain: that whatsoever ye shall ask
of the Father in my name, he may give it you.
17These things I command you, that ye love
one another.

The disciples warned of persecution

[18]If the world hate you, ye know that it hated
me before *it hated* you. [19]If ye were of the
world, the world would love his own: but
because ye are not of the world, but I have
chosen you out of the world, therefore the
world hateth you. [20]Remember the word that
I said unto you, The servant is not greater
than his lord. If they have persecuted me,
they will also persecute you; if they have kept
my saying, they will keep your's also. [21]But
all these things will they do unto you for my
name's sake, because they know not him that
sent me. [22]If I had not come and spoken unto
them, they had not had sin: but now they
have no cloke for their sin. [23]He that hateth
me hateth my Father also. [24]If I had not done
among them the works which none other
man did, they had not had sin: but now have
they both seen and hated both me and my
Father. [25]But *this cometh to pass*, that the word
might be fulfilled that is written in their law,
They hated me without a cause. (*Psalm 69.4*).

26 But when the Comforter is come, whom
I will send unto you from the Father, *even*
the Spirit of truth, which proceedeth from the
Father, he shall testify of me: 27 And ye also
shall bear witness, because ye have been with
me from the beginning.

The Spirit of Truth, the Comforter

16 These things have I spoken unto you,
that ye should not be offended. 2 They
shall put you out of the synagogues: yea, the
time cometh, that whosoever killeth you will
think that he doeth God service. 3 And these
things will they do unto you, because they
have not known the Father, nor me. 4 But
these things have I told you, that when the
time shall come, ye may remember that I told
you of them. And these things I said not unto
you at the beginning, because I was with you.
5 But now I go my way to him that sent me;
and none of you asketh me, Whither goest
thou? 6 But because I have said these things
unto you, sorrow hath filled your heart.

7 Nevertheless I tell you the truth; It is ex-
pedient for you that I go away: for if I go not
away, the Comforter will not come unto you;
but if I depart, I will send him unto you.
8 And when he is come, he will reprove the
world of sin, and of righteousness, and of
judgment: 9 Of sin, because they believe not
on me; 10 Of righteousness, because I go to my
Father, and ye see me no more; 11 Of judg-
ment, because the prince of this world is
judged.

12 I have yet many things to say unto you,
but ye cannot bear them now. 13 Howbeit when
he, the Spirit of truth, is come, he will guide
you into all truth: for he shall not speak of
himself; but whatsoever he shall hear, *that*
shall he speak: and he will shew you things
to come. 14 He shall glorify me: for he shall
receive of mine, and shall shew *it* unto you.
15 All things that the Father hath are mine:
therefore said I, that he shall take of mine, and
shall shew *it* unto you.

16 A little while, and ye shall not see me:

and again, a little while, and ye shall see me,
because I go to the Father. 17Then said *some*
of his disciples among themselves, What is
this that he saith unto us, A little while, and
ye shall not see me: and again, a little while,
and ye shall see me: and, Because I go to the
Father? 18They said therefore, What is this
that he saith, A little while? we cannot tell
what he saith.

19Now Jesus knew that they were desirous
to ask him, and said unto them, Do ye en-
quire among yourselves of that I said, A little
while, and ye shall not see me: and again, a
little while, and ye shall see me? 20Verily,
verily, I say unto you, That ye shall weep and
lament, but the world shall rejoice: and ye
shall be sorrowful, but your sorrow shall be
turned into joy. 21A woman when she is in
travail hath sorrow, because her hour is come:
but as soon as she is delivered of the child, she
remembereth no more the anguish, for joy
that a man is born into the world. 22And ye
now therefore have sorrow: but I will see you

again, and your heart shall rejoice, and your
joy no man taketh from you. 23 And in that day
ye shall ask me nothing. Verily, verily, I say
unto you, Whatsoever ye shall ask the Father
in my name, he will give *it* you. 24 Hitherto
have ye asked nothing in my name: ask, and
ye shall receive, that your joy may be full.

The disciples are encouraged to pray

25 These things have I spoken unto you in
proverbs: but the time cometh, when I shall
no more speak unto you in proverbs, but I
shall shew you plainly of the Father. 26 At that
day ye shall ask in my name: and I say not
unto you, that I will pray the Father for you:
27 For the Father himself loveth you, because
ye have loved me, and have believed that I
came out from God. 28 I came forth from the
Father, and am come into the world: again, I
leave the world, and go to the Father.

29 His disciples said unto him, Lo, now
speakest thou plainly, and speakest no pro-
verb. 30 Now are we sure that thou knowest all

things, and needest not that any man should
ask thee: by this we believe that thou camest
forth from God. 31 Jesus answered them, Do ye
now believe? 32 Behold, the hour cometh, yea,
is now come, that ye shall be scattered, every
man to his own, and shall leave me alone:
and yet I am not alone, because the Father is
with me. 33 These things I have spoken unto
you, that in me ye might have peace. In the
world ye shall have tribulation: but be of good
cheer; I have overcome the world.

Jesus prays to His Father

17 These words spake Jesus, and lifted
up his eyes to heaven, and said,
Father, the hour is come; glorify thy Son,
that thy Son also may glorify thee: 2 As thou
hast given him power over all flesh, that he
should give eternal life to as many as thou
hast given him. 3 And this is life eternal, that
they might know thee the only true God, and
Jesus Christ, whom thou hast sent. 4 I have
glorified thee on the earth: I have finished the

work which thou gavest me to do. 5 And now,
O Father, glorify thou me with thine own self
with the glory which I had with thee before
the world was.

6 I have manifested thy name unto the men
which thou gavest me out of the world: thine
they were, and thou gavest them me; and
they have kept thy word. 7 Now they have
known that all things whatsoever thou hast
given me are of thee. 8 For I have given unto
them the words which thou gavest me; and
they have received *them*, and have known
surely that I came out from thee, and they
have believed that thou didst send me.

9 I pray for them: I pray not for the world,
but for them which thou hast given me; for
they are thine. 10 And all mine are thine, and
thine are mine; and I am glorified in them.
11 And now I am no more in the world, but
these are in the world, and I come to thee.
Holy Father, keep through thine own name
those whom thou hast given me, that they
may be one, as we *are*. 12 While I was with

them in the world, I kept them in thy name:
those that thou gavest me I have kept, and
none of them is lost, but the son of perdition;
that the scripture might be fulfilled.

[13]And now come I to thee; and these things
I speak in the world, that they might have my
joy fulfilled in themselves. [14]I have given
them thy word; and the world hath hated
them, because they are not of the world, even
as I am not of the world. [15]I pray not that thou
shouldest take them out of the world, but that
thou shouldest keep them from the evil. [16]They
are not of the world, even as I am not of the
world. [17]Sanctify them through thy truth: thy
word is truth. [18]As thou hast sent me into the
world, even so have I also sent them into the
world. [19]And for their sakes I sanctify myself,
that they also might be sanctified through the
truth.

[20]Neither pray I for these alone, but for
them also which shall believe on me through
their word; [21]That they all may be one; as
thou, Father, *art* in me, and I in thee, that

they also may be one in us: that the world may
believe that thou hast sent me. [22]And the
glory which thou gavest me I have given
them; that they may be one, even as we are
one: [23]I in them, and thou in me, that they
may be made perfect in one; and that the
world may know that thou hast sent me, and
hast loved them, as thou hast loved me.
[24]Father, I will that they also, whom thou
hast given me, be with me where I am; that
they may behold my glory, which thou hast
given me: for thou lovedst me before the
foundation of the world.
[25]O righteous Father, the world hath not
known thee: but I have known thee, and
these have known that thou hast sent me,
[26]And I have declared unto them thy name.
and will declare *it:* that the love wherewith
thou hast loved me may be in them, and I in
them.

The betrayal and denial

18 When Jesus had spoken these words, he went forth with his disciples over the brook Cedron, where was a garden, into the which he entered, and his disciples.

2 And Judas also, which betrayed him, knew
the place: for Jesus ofttimes resorted thither
with his disciples. 3 Judas then, having re-
ceived a band *of men* and officers from the
chief priests and Pharisees, cometh thither
with lanterns and torches and weapons.

4 Jesus therefore, knowing all things that
should come upon him, went forth, and said
unto them, Whom seek ye? 5 They answered
him, Jesus of Nazareth. Jesus saith unto them,
I am *he*. And Judas also, which betrayed him,
stood with them. 6 As soon then as he had said
unto them, I am *he*, they went backward, and
fell to the ground.

7 Then asked he them again, Whom seek
ye? And they said, Jesus of Nazareth. 8 Jesus
answered, I have told you that I am *he:* if
therefore ye seek me, let these go their way:

9 That the saying might be fulfilled, which he
spake, Of them which thou gavest me have I
lost none.
10 Then Simon Peter having a sword drew
it, and smote the high priest's servant, and
cut off his right ear. The servant's name was
Malchus. 11 Then said Jesus unto Peter, Put
up thy sword into the sheath: the cup which
my Father hath given me, shall I not drink it?
12 Then the band and the captain and officers
of the Jews took Jesus, and bound him, 13 And
led him away to Annas first; for he was father
in law to Caiaphas, which was the high priest
that same year. 14 Now Caiaphas was he, which
gave counsel to the Jews, that it was expedient
that one man should die for the people.
15 And Simon Peter followed Jesus, and *so
did* another disciple: that disciple was known
unto the high priest, and went in with Jesus
into the palace of the high priest. 16 But Peter
stood at the door without. Then went out that
other disciple, which was known unto the
high priest, and spake unto her that kept the

door, and brought in Peter. 17 Then saith the
damsel that kept the door unto Peter, Art not
thou also *one* of this man's disciples? He saith,
I am not. 18 And the servants and officers stood
there, who had made a fire of coals; for it was
cold: and they warmed themselves: and Peter
stood with them, and warmed himself.

Jesus brought before the High Priest

19 The high priest then asked Jesus of his
disciples, and of his doctrine. 20 Jesus an-
swered him, I spake openly to the world; I
ever taught in the synagogue, and in the
temple, whither the Jews always resort; and in
secret have I said nothing. 21 Why askest thou
me? ask them which heard me, what I have
said unto them: behold, they know what I said.

22 And when he had thus spoken, one of the
officers which stood by struck Jesus with the
palm of his hand, saying, Answerest thou the
high priest so? 23 Jesus answered him, If I
have spoken evil, bear witness of the evil:
but if well, why smitest thou me?

[24]Now Annas had sent him bound unto
Caiaphas the high priest.
[25]And Simon Peter stood and warmed him-
self. They said therefore unto him, Art not
thou also *one* of his disciples? He denied *it*,
and said, I am not. [26]One of the servants of
the high priest, being *his* kinsman whose ear
Peter cut off, saith, Did not I see thee in the
garden with him? [27]Peter then denied again:
and immediately the cock crew.

Jesus before Pilate

[28]Then led they Jesus from Caiaphas unto
the hall of judgment: and it was early; and
they themselves went not into the judgment
hall, lest they should be defiled; but that they
might eat the passover. [29]Pilate then went out
unto them, and said, What accusation bring
ye against this man? [30]They answered and
said unto him, If he were not a malefactor, we
would not have delivered him up unto thee.
[31]Then said Pilate unto them, Take ye him,
and judge him according to your law. The

Jews therefore said unto him, It is not lawful
for us to put any man to death: 32That the
saying of Jesus might be fulfilled, which he
spake, signifying what death he should die.

33Then Pilate entered into the judgment
hall again, and called Jesus, and said unto
him, Art thou the King of the Jews? 34Jesus
answered him, Sayest thou this thing of thy-
self, or did others tell it thee of me? 35Pilate
answered, Am I a Jew? Thine own nation
and the chief priests have delivered thee unto
me: what hast thou done? 36Jesus answered,
My kingdom is not of this world: if my king-
dom were of this world, then would my ser-
vants fight, that I should not be delivered to
the Jews: but now is my kingdom not from
hence. 37Pilate therefore said unto him, Art
thou a king then? Jesus answered, Thou say-
est that I am a king. To this end was I born,
and for this cause came I into the world, that
I should bear witness unto the truth. Every
one that is of the truth heareth my voice.
38Pilate saith unto him, What is truth?

And when he had said this, he went out
again unto the Jews, and saith unto them, I
find in him no fault *at all.* 39But ye have a
custom, that I should release unto you one at
the passover: will ye therefore that I release
unto you the King of the Jews? 40Then cried
they all again, saying, Not this man, but
Barabbas. Now Barabbas was a robber.

The crucifixion, death, and burial

19 Then Pilate therefore took Jesus, and
scourged *him.* 2And the soldiers plat-
ted a crown of thorns, and put *it* on his head,
and they put on him a purple robe, 3And said,
Hail, King of the Jews! and they smote him
with their hands. (*Isaiah 53.3, 5, 7*).

4Pilate therefore went forth again, and saith
unto them, Behold, I bring him forth to you,
that ye may know that I find no fault in him.
5Then came Jesus forth, wearing the crown
of thorns, and the purple robe. And *Pilate*
saith unto them, Behold the man!

6When the chief priests therefore and offi-

cers saw him, they cried out, saying, Crucify
him, crucify *him*. Pilate saith unto them, Take
ye him, and crucify *him:* for I find no fault in
him. 7The Jews answered him, We have a law,
and by our law he ought to die, because he
made himself the Son of God.

8When Pilate therefore heard that saying,
he was the more afraid; 9And went again into
the judgment hall, and saith unto Jesus,
Whence art thou? But Jesus gave him no
answer. 10Then saith Pilate unto him, Speak-
est thou not unto me? knowest thou not that
I have power to crucify thee, and have power
to release thee? 11Jesus answered, Thou could-
est have no power *at all* against me, except it
were given thee from above: therefore he that
delivered me unto thee hath the greater sin.

12And from thenceforth Pilate sought to re-
lease him: but the Jews cried out, saying, If
thou let this man go, thou art not Cæsar's
friend: whosoever maketh himself a king
speaketh against Cæsar.

13When Pilate therefore heard that saying,

he brought Jesus forth, and sat down in the
judgment seat in a place that is called the
Pavement, but in the Hebrew, Gabbatha.
[14]And it was the preparation of the passover,
and about the sixth hour: and he saith unto
the Jews, Behold your King! [15]But they cried
out, Away with *him*, away with *him*, crucify
him. Pilate saith unto them, Shall I crucify
your King? The chief priests answered, We
have no king but Cæsar. [16]Then delivered he
him therefore unto them to be crucified. And
they took Jesus, and led *him* away.

[17]And he bearing his cross went forth into
a place called *the place* of a skull, which is
called in the Hebrew Golgotha: [18]Where they
crucified him, and two other with him, on
either side one, and Jesus in the midst. (*Isaiah
53.12*).

[19]And Pilate wrote a title, and put *it* on the
cross. And the writing was, JESUS OF NA-
ZARETH THE KING OF THE JEWS.
[20]This title then read many of the Jews: for
the place where Jesus was crucified was nigh

to the city: and it was written in Hebrew, *and*
Greek, *and* Latin. 21Then said the chief priests
of the Jews to Pilate, Write not, The King of
the Jews; but that he said, I am King of the
Jews. 22Pilate answered, What I have written
I have written.

23Then the soldiers, when they had crucified
Jesus, took his garments, and made four parts,
to every soldier a part; and also *his* coat: now
the coat was without seam, woven from the
top throughout. 24They said therefore among
themselves, Let us not rend it, but cast lots
for it, whose it shall be: that the scripture
might be fulfilled, which saith, They parted
my raiment among them, and for my vesture
they did cast lots. (*Psalm 22.18*). These
things therefore the soldiers did.

25Now there stood by the cross of Jesus his
mother, and his mother's sister, Mary the
wife of Cleophas, and Mary Magdalene.
26When Jesus therefore saw his mother, and
the disciple standing by, whom he loved, he
saith unto his mother, Woman, behold thy

son! 27Then saith he to the disciple, Behold
thy mother! And from that hour that disciple
took her unto his own *home*.

28After this, Jesus knowing that all things
were now accomplished, that the scripture
might be fulfilled, saith, I thirst. 29Now there
was set a vessel full of vinegar: and they filled
a spunge with vinegar, and put *it* upon hyssop,
and put *it* to his mouth. (*Psalm 69.21*). 30When
Jesus therefore had received the vinegar, he
said, It is finished: and he bowed his head,
and gave up the ghost.

31The Jews therefore, because it was the
preparation, that the bodies should not re-
main upon the cross on the sabbath day, (for
that sabbath day was an high day,) besought
Pilate that their legs might be broken, and
that they might be taken away. 32Then came
the soldiers, and brake the legs of the first,
and of the other which was crucified with him.

33But when they came to Jesus, and saw
that he was dead already, they brake not his

legs: 34 But one of the soldiers with a spear
pierced his side, and forthwith came there
out blood and water. 35 And he that saw *it* bare
record, and his record is true: and he knoweth
that he saith true, that ye might believe. 36 For
these things were done, that the scripture
should be fulfilled, A bone of him shall not
be broken. 37 And again another scripture
saith, They shall look on him whom they
pierced. (*Numbers 9.12; Zechariah 12.10*).

38 And after this Joseph of Arimathæa, being
a disciple of Jesus, but secretly for fear of the
Jews, besought Pilate that he might take away
the body of Jesus: and Pilate gave *him* leave.
He came therefore, and took the body of
Jesus. 39 And there came also Nicodemus,
which at the first came to Jesus by night, and
brought a mixture of myrrh and aloes, about
an hundred pound *weight*. 40 Then took they
the body of Jesus, and wound it in linen
clothes with the spices, as the manner of the
Jews is to bury.

41 Now in the place where he was crucified
there was a garden; and in the garden a new
sepulchre, wherein was never man yet laid.
42 There laid they Jesus therefore because of
the Jews' preparation *day;* for the sepulchre
was nigh at hand.

The Risen Lord

20 The first *day* of the week cometh
Mary Magdalene early, when it was
yet dark, unto the sepulchre, and seeth the
stone taken away from the sepulchre. 2 Then
she runneth, and cometh to Simon Peter, and
to the other disciple, whom Jesus loved, and
saith unto them, They have taken away the
Lord out of the sepulchre, and we know not
where they have laid him.

3 Peter therefore went forth, and that other
disciple, and came to the sepulchre. 4 So they
ran both together: and the other disciple did
outrun Peter, and came first to the sepulchre.
5 And he stooping down, *and looking in,* saw
the linen clothes lying; yet went he not in.

6Then cometh Simon Peter following him,
and went into the sepulchre, and seeth the
linen clothes lie, 7And the napkin, that was
about his head, not lying with the linen
clothes, but wrapped together in a place by
itself. 8Then went in also that other disciple,
which came first to the sepulchre, and he
saw, and believed. 9For as yet they knew not
the scripture, that he must rise again from the
dead. (*Psalm 16.10*). 10Then the disciples
went away again unto their own home.

11But Mary stood without at the sepulchre
weeping: and as she wept, she stooped down,
and looked into the sepulchre, 12And seeth
two angels in white sitting, the one at the
head, and the other at the feet, where the body
of Jesus had lain. 13And they say unto her,
Woman, why weepest thou? She saith unto
them, Because they have taken away my Lord,
and I know not where they have laid him.

14And when she had thus said, she turned
herself back, and saw Jesus standing, and
knew not that it was Jesus. 15Jesus saith unto

her, Woman, why weepest thou? whom seek-
est thou? She, supposing him to be the gar-
dener, saith unto him, Sir, if thou have borne
him hence, tell me where thou hast laid him,
and I will take him away. [16]Jesus saith unto
her, Mary. She turned herself, and saith unto
him, Rabboni; which is to say, Master.

[17]Jesus saith unto her, Touch me not; for I
am not yet ascended to my Father: but go to
my brethren, and say unto them, I ascend unto
my Father, and your Father; and *to* my God,
and your God. [18]Mary Magdalene came and
told the disciples that she had seen the Lord,
and *that* he had spoken these things unto her.

[19]Then the same day at evening, being the
first *day* of the week, when the doors were
shut where the disciples were assembled for
fear of the Jews, came Jesus and stood in the
midst, and saith unto them, Peace *be* unto
you. [20]And when he had so said, he shewed
unto them *his* hands and his side. Then were
the disciples glad, when they saw the Lord.

21 Then said Jesus to them again, Peace *be*
unto you: as *my* Father hath sent me, even so
send I you. 22 And when he had said this, he
breathed on *them*, and saith unto them, Re-
ceive ye the Holy Ghost: 23 Whose soever sins
ye remit, they are remitted unto them; *and*
whose soever *sins* ye retain, they are retained.

24 But Thomas, one of the twelve, called
Didymus, was not with them when Jesus
came. 25 The other disciples therefore said un-
to him, We have seen the Lord. But he said
unto them, Except I shall see in his hands
the print of the nails, and put my finger into
the print of the nails, and thrust my hand
into his side, I will not believe.

26 And after eight days again his disciples
were within, and Thomas with them: *then*
came Jesus, the doors being shut, and stood
in the midst, and said, Peace *be* unto you.
27 Then saith he to Thomas, Reach hither thy
finger, and behold my hands; and reach
hither thy hand, and thrust *it* into my side:
and be not faithless, but believing. 28 And

Thomas answered and said unto him, My
Lord and my God. 29Jesus saith unto him,
Thomas, because thou hast seen me, thou
hast believed: blessed *are* they that have not
seen, and *yet* have believed.

30And many other signs truly did Jesus in
the presence of his disciples, which are not
written in this book: 31But these are written,
that ye might believe that Jesus is the Christ,
the Son of God; and that believing ye might
have life through his name. (*Psalm 2.7, 12*).

21 After these things Jesus shewed him-
self again to the disciples at the sea of
Tiberias; and on this wise shewed he *himself*.
2There were together Simon Peter, and
Thomas called Didymus, and Nathanael of
Cana in Galilee, and the *sons* of Zebedee, and
two other of his disciples. 3Simon Peter saith
unto them, I go a fishing. They say unto him,
We also go with thee. They went forth, and
entered into a ship immediately; and that
night they caught nothing.

4But when the morning was now come,
Jesus stood on the shore: but the disciples
knew not that it was Jesus. 5Then Jesus saith
unto them, Children, have ye any meat? They
answered him, No. 6And he said unto them,
Cast the net on the right side of the ship, and
ye shall find. They cast therefore, and now
they were not able to draw it for the multitude
of fishes.

7Therefore that disciple whom Jesus loved
saith unto Peter, It is the Lord. Now when
Simon Peter heard that it was the Lord, he
girt *his* fisher's coat *unto him*, (for he was
naked,) and did cast himself into the sea.
8And the other disciples came in a little ship;
(for they were not far from land, but as it
were two hundred cubits,) dragging the net
with fishes.

9As soon then as they were come to land,
they saw a fire of coals there, and fish laid
thereon, and bread. 10Jesus saith unto them,
Bring of the fish which ye have now caught.
11Simon Peter went up, and drew the net to

land full of great fishes, an hundred and fifty
and three: and for all there were so many, yet
was not the net broken.
[12]Jesus saith unto them, Come *and* dine.
And none of the disciples durst ask him,
Who art thou? knowing that it was the Lord.
[13]Jesus then cometh, and taketh bread, and
giveth them, and fish likewise. [14]This is now
the third time that Jesus shewed himself to
his disciples, after that he was risen from the
dead.

[15]So when they had dined, Jesus saith to
Simon Peter, Simon, *son* of Jonas, lovest thou
me more than these? He saith unto him, Yea,
Lord; thou knowest that I love thee. He saith
unto him, Feed my lambs. [16]He saith to him
again the second time, Simon, *son* of Jonas,
lovest thou me? He saith unto him, Yea,
Lord; thou knowest that I love thee. He saith
unto him, Feed my sheep. [17]He saith unto
him the third time, Simon, *son* of Jonas,
lovest thou me? Peter was grieved because

he said unto him the third time, Lovest thou
me? And he said unto him, Lord, thou know-
est all things; thou knowest that I love thee.
Jesus saith unto him, Feed my sheep. [18]Verily,
verily, I say unto thee, When thou wast young,
thou girdedst thyself, and walkedst whither
thou wouldest: but when thou shalt be old,
thou shalt stretch forth thy hands, and another
shall gird thee, and carry *thee* whither thou
wouldest not. [19]This spake he, signifying by
what death he should glorify God. And when
he had spoken this, he saith unto him, Follow
me.

[20]Then Peter, turning about, seeth the dis-
ciple whom Jesus loved following; which also
leaned on his breast at supper, and said,
Lord, which is he that betrayeth thee? [21]Peter
seeing him saith to Jesus, Lord, and what
shall this man *do?* [22]Jesus saith unto him, If I
will that he tarry till I come, what *is that* to
thee? follow thou me.

[23]Then went this saying abroad among the
brethren, that that disciple should not die:

yet Jesus said not unto him, He shall not die;
but, If I will that he tarry till I come, what *is*
that to thee?
24 This is the disciple which testifieth of
these things, and wrote these things: and we
know that his testimony is true.
25 And there are also many other things
which Jesus did, the which, if they should be
written every one, I suppose that even the
world itself could not contain the books that
should be written. Amen.

Index

INDEX